GCSE English Literature
Revise
Macbeth
Model Answers and Practice
from
GCSEEnglish.uk

Edward Mooney

gcseenglish.uk

First Printing: 2023

ISBN 979-8768277819

www.gcseenglish.uk

Contents

Introduction	**1**
1: Ambition	**5**
2: The supernatural	**9**
3: A violent character	**15**
4: A changing female character	**19**
5: A powerful woman	**25**
6: A hero	**29**
7: Marriage	**33**
8: The Macduffs	**39**
9: Appearances and reality	**43**
10: Good and evil	**49**
11: Natural and unnatural	**53**
12: Guilt	**59**
Appendix 1: How will my essay be assessed?	**65**

Introduction

In this book, you will find the guidance you need to help you improve your *Macbeth* essay writing for the AQA GCSE English Literature exam.

There are practice exam-style essay tasks, essay writing checklists and complete full-marks model answers to help show you what a good essay looks like and what the examiners are looking for. All the tasks are based on recent, publicly available past papers.

Essay writing is a very important part of the English curriculum and is assessed extensively at GCSE; the AQA *Macbeth* assessment represents 21% of your total GCSE English Literature grade. Regular practice of essay writing is therefore vital for boosting exam grades.

Regular essay writing practice will also help boost your knowledge of the text.

How to use this book

There are a range of different ways you can use this book. You could:

- read the essays and see what an excellent exam answer looks like.
- read the exam tasks and then plan and write your own essays.
- use the checklists (provided after every essay) to see how many of the writing recommendations are met by each essay.
- use the checklists (provided after every essay) to help you plan and write your own essays.
- read the essays again, more slowly, identifying, and remembering, key interpretations of *Macbeth*.
- re-write the essays using different textual evidence and/or a differing set of interpretations.

Of course, these are practice tasks and model answers. Your writing in your exam should be your own work. Don't attempt to memorise an essay and copy it out as you risk being penalised, such as having marks taken away or even being disqualified from the entire exam.

About Interpretation of Text and Context

Interpretation of literary texts and contexts can differ from person to person. You may read interpretations here that are new to you or perhaps you may even disagree with some of the interpretations. This is to be expected, and especially so with Shakespeare as there is a long history of sometimes wildly differing interpretations and, indeed, an entire 'bard industry' dedicated to re-thinking, re-imagining, re-examining Shakespeare.

Clearly controversy rages about Shakespeare, even about his very existence, but my recommendation is to leave the controversy to the academics. Learning about the less mainstream interpretations, while fascinating, is proper for A Level students and higher. The assessment objectives at GCSE do not ask for 'other interpretations' as is common on A Level exam specifications. (See Appendix 1 for more information on assessment objectives.)

To help you navigate this disorientating web of interpretation, I have kept the interpretations in these essays very close to the mainstream interpretations offered by three common textbooks used in many classrooms (see below). I have also made extensive use of the interpretations identified as top band indicative content in exam board mark schemes, exemplars and training material. My reasonable assumption is: if it is in the mark scheme then it should be in the essay.

If the mainstream interpretations change (which is entirely possible), then I will update the essays in future editions.

Having noted all this, if you feel inspired to dig deeper into the complex world of different interpretations of Shakespeare, please do. I especially encourage you to watch recent theatre and film adaptations of *Macbeth* as these will best demonstrate what are the currently fashionable interpretations of the text and will also be excellent learning opportunities.

Texts

There are many different versions of *Macbeth* and many different study aids available. I have worked with the versions below:

- *Oxford School Shakespeare: Macbeth*. ISBN: 978-0198324003. https://amzn.to/3q4wPiD (All quotations and act/scene/line references are taken from this text.)
- *Macbeth (Cambridge School Shakespeare)*. ISBN: 978-1107615496. https://amzn.to/3q4hPkQ
- *GCSE English Literature for AQA Macbeth Student Book (GCSE English Literature AQA)*. ISBN: 978-1107453951. https://amzn.to/3HL1G9P

I have included act/scene/line references to help with your revision. However, there is no requirement to include these references in your exam essay.

More about me

I am a qualified teacher of English with a degree in English Literature from the University of Cambridge. I have taught and examined GCSE and A Level English courses at outstanding schools since 2006. I now write model answers and provide exam preparation through my website gcseenglish.uk.

Keep up to date with future projects and collections of model answers by subscribing to my newsletter or by following my social media channels. Visit gcseenglish.uk or search gcseenglishuk and feel free to leave a review.

Best of luck in your exams!

1: Ambition

Read the following extract from Act 1 Scene 5 of *Macbeth* and then answer the question that follows.

At this point in the play, Lady Macbeth is speaking. She has just read Macbeth's letter telling her about his meeting with the three witches.

LADY MACBETH
Glamis thou art, and Cawdor, and shalt be
What thou art promis'd; yet do I fear thy nature,
It is too full o'th'milk of human kindness
To catch the nearest way. Thou wouldst be great,
Art not without ambition, but without
The illness should attend it. What thou wouldst highly,
That wouldst thou holily; wouldst not play false,
And yet wouldst wrongly win. Thou'dst have, great Glamis,
That which cries, 'Thus thou must do' if thou have it;
And that which rather thou dost fear to do,
Than wishest should be undone. Hie thee hither,
That I may pour my spirits in thine ear
And chastise with the valour of my tongue
All that impedes thee from the golden round,
Which fate and metaphysical aid doth seem
To have thee crown'd withal.

Starting with this speech, explore how Shakespeare presents ambition in *Macbeth*.

Write about:

- how Shakespeare presents ambition in this speech
- how Shakespeare presents ambition in the play as a whole.

1: The Essay

In *Macbeth*, Shakespeare presents ambition as the tragic flaw that causes Macbeth's downfall. In the extract, Lady Macbeth questions Macbeth's *lack* of ambition and she resolves to persuade him to seize the throne. Later, Shakespeare shows how Macbeth's ambition is encouraged by the Witches' prophecies and by his own desire for power as we see him transformed from a loyal subject, to a murderous tyrant, to a defeated usurper. Performed before King James VI and I in 1606, the play suggests, presumably to the satisfaction of the king, that ambitious rebels against divinely appointed kings should expect gruesome punishment.

In Lady Macbeth's soliloquy, Shakespeare presents ambition as something that Macbeth lacks, suggesting that Lady Macbeth aims to manipulate Macbeth to take action. Alone, Lady Macbeth speaks her true thoughts aloud, fearing that Macbeth is "too full o'th'milk of human kindness to catch the nearest way" to the throne (1.5.16-17). The milk symbolism is an insult, suggesting that Lady Macbeth feels that her husband is too feminine. Ambition, here, is clearly linked to masculinity and the original audience may well have been shocked to see a female character being so openly ambitious, thereby transgressing traditional norms of female behaviour. Lady Macbeth then argues that ambition requires "illness" (1.5.19), in order to bear fruit. This suggests that she appears to believe that masculine cruelty is necessary to be great and, indeed, she later calls on supernatural power to "unsex" (1.5.40) her and make her cruel. This is perhaps an echo of Machiavelli's notorious advice to princes that vice should be used in order to get and retain power. Lady Macbeth concludes by resolving to give Macbeth her qualities through the power of her rhetoric: "I may pour my spirits in thine ear." (1.5.25) The metaphor presents persuasion as a fluid, filling Macbeth's head with something unnatural and deadly.

Although Lady Macbeth dismisses Macbeth's lack of ambition, Shakespeare presents ambition as an important motivation for Macbeth. Soon after meeting the Witches, Banquo notices that Macbeth is "rapt" (1.3.55 and 1.3.141). Macbeth seems to be already imagining his royal future. Later, when Duncan proclaims Malcom as his heir, Macbeth reveals his "black and deep desires" (1.4.51). Whispering to himself, he uses imagery of darkness to emphasise how disturbing his ambition is and to reveal his plan to "o'erleap" (1.4.48-49) Malcolm. This access to Macbeth's thoughts sets up a dramatically ironic scene where Macbeth simultaneously proclaims his loyalty and signals his treachery. However, Macbeth is never firm in his resolve and almost abandons the murder noting his "vaulting ambition which o'erleaps itself." (1.7.27-28) Here he imagines ambition as a horse failing to jump a fence. This wavering is ended by Lady Macbeth's mockery ("Wouldst thou...live a coward?" [1.7.41-43]) and we see that, without her ambition, Macbeth's ambition may have withered away. This reflects the source, *The Chronicles of Scotland*, in which the killing of Duncan is a product of both Macbeth's ambition and Lady Macbeth's "unquenchable desire" to be queen (p102).

Shakespeare later presents ambition as a character flaw that causes Macbeth's downfall. Upon becoming king, Macbeth mourns his "fruitless crown." (3.1.62). This ambition to father a dynasty, expressed using metaphors of infertility, causes him to plot to have Banquo and his son Fleance, prophesied by the witches to "get kings" (1.3.65), killed. Their continued existence eats away at Macbeth and he exclaims: "full of scorpions is my mind." (3.2.36) This metaphor suggests that Macbeth is poisoned by his ambition and that it is causing him pain and indeed, when Macbeth learns that Fleance has escaped he cries out: "then comes my fit again." (3.4.21) This is the beginning of Macbeth's downfall. Later, as the army advances, Macbeth reaches a moment of nihilistic realisation proclaiming that life is "a tale told by an idiot...signifying nothing." (5.5.25-27) Shakespeare shows that ambition leads only to destruction and meaninglessness. The arrival of the rightful heir represents a return to the correct "measure, time and place," (5.9.40) and perhaps reflects contemporary discussions about the Divine Right of Kings; Macbeth's ambition causes him to outrage God and he receives his just punishment.

Thus, in *Macbeth*, Shakespeare presents ambition as a disruptive force that undermines duty and loyalty, usurps legitimate leaders and leads, ultimately, to the just death of the usurper. Moreover, ambition is presented as an illness and as a character flaw that brings about the tragic hero's destruction. Then, as in many other tragedies, a new equilibrium of peace and good order dawns. Though twenty-first century audiences may have a more positive view of ambition, the play still resonates as a powerful depiction of how *excessive* ambition and absolute power can corrupt previously virtuous people.

1: Essay Writing Checklist

As you read, check how many of the recommendations below are followed by the essay. Then, use the checklist to help you write your own essay.

Remember that these are *recommendations* from an experienced teacher, not *requirements*. Allow them to help and guide you, but don't allow them to restrict you; if you have a different idea and feel confident about it, then give it a go!

- ☐ Use wording of question in answer – "Shakespeare presents."
- ☐ Use Intro and Conclusion to help structure essay as argument.
- ☐ Use topic sentences to open each main paragraph.
- ☐ Close focus on extract.
- ☐ Focus on elsewhere in the play.
- ☐ Use short, precise quotations to support interpretations.
- ☐ Close analysis of language, especially aspects of poetry.
- ☐ Close analysis of form, especially aspects of performance.
- ☐ Close analysis of text structure, especially aspects of tragedy.
- ☐ Refer to effect on audience.
- ☐ Use relevant subject terminology.
- ☐ Connect to context when text was written, where relevant: Jacobean era.
- ☐ Connect to context when text is set, where relevant: early medieval Scotland.
- ☐ Connect to literary context, where relevant: history of the genre of tragedy.
- ☐ Connect to original and 21st century audience context, where relevant.
- ☐ Focus on minor character(s), where relevant.
- ☐ Use accurate spelling, punctuation and grammar.
- ☐ Write c450-c750 words.

2: The supernatural

Read the following extract from Act 1 Scene 3 of *Macbeth* and then answer the question that follows.

At this point in the play, after receiving The Witches' prophecies, Macbeth and Banquo have just been told that Duncan has made Macbeth Thane of Cawdor.

BANQUO

But 'tis strange,
And oftentimes, to win us to our harm,
The instruments of darkness tell us truths;
Win us with honest trifles, to betray's
In deepest consequence. –
Cousins, a word, I pray you.

MACBETH [Aside]

Two truths are told,
As happy prologues to the swelling act
Of the imperial theme. – I thank you, gentlemen. –
This supernatural soliciting
Cannot be ill, cannot be good. If ill,
Why hath it given me earnest of success,
Commencing in a truth? I am Thane of Cawdor.
If good, why do I yield to that suggestion,
Whose horrid image doth unfix my hair
And make my seated heart knock at my ribs
Against the use of nature? Present fears
Are less than horrible imaginings.
My thought, whose murder yet is but fantastical,
Shakes so my single state of man that function
Is smother'd in surmise, and nothing is,
But what is not.

Starting with this moment in the play, explore how Shakespeare presents the attitudes of Macbeth and Banquo towards the supernatural.

Write about:

- how Shakespeare presents the attitudes of Macbeth and Banquo towards the supernatural in this extract
- how Shakespeare presents the attitudes of Macbeth and Banquo towards the supernatural in the play as a whole.

2: The Essay

Shakespeare presents Macbeth and Banquo's attitudes towards the supernatural as fear tinged with tentative credulity. In the extract, Banquo warns Macbeth about the devious ways of supernatural beings. Macbeth, by contrast, is excited by the prophecies. Elsewhere in the play, Shakespeare shows how Macbeth is guided to kill Duncan by a supernatural vision. By the end, Macbeth, poisoned by his trust in the supernatural, believes himself to be invincible and dies a traitor's death. Performed in an era of witch trials, the play suggests, just as the witchfinders did, that the world of the supernatural is real but it should be rejected and destroyed.

In the extract, Shakespeare presents contrasting attitudes to the supernatural. Banquo is nervous and recommends that he and Macbeth be wary of the Witches' intent, arguing that they aim to "win us to our harm" (1.3.122) after initially beguiling them. He then immediately moves away from where the Witches appeared, showing us that Banquo is sensible, refusing to be taken in. Macbeth, now isolated on stage, thereby emphasising a contrast, has a completely different attitude. Whispering to himself, he imagines himself as king, considering the "happy prologues...of the imperial theme." (1.3.127-128) This metaphor seems to show Macbeth thinking of the myths that will be told after his death and suggests he is no longer in the world of facts and reason. In fact, he then attempts to reason with himself, wondering if these supernatural visitations "cannot be ill, cannot be good" (1.3.130) but his arguments create a see-saw of contradictions and he is "smother'd in surmise." (1.3.140) This metaphor suggests that the Witches have suffocated Macbeth; they have 'won' him. This depiction of the Witches reflects Jacobean attitudes: witches were considered to be real beings who could use magic to enthral and destroy.

Later, Shakespeare presents Macbeth and Banquo continuing to respond in contrasting ways to the supernatural. Moments before killing Duncan, Macbeth sees a vision of a bloody dagger. He questions its existence and dismisses it as a "false creation." (2.1.38) Despite this apparent scepticism, however, Macbeth proceeds to kill Duncan, fulfilling the Witches' second prophecy. This suggests that Macbeth is ready to believe in, and be guided by, the supernatural. After Macbeth's coronation, Banquo's scepticism increases as he wonders, to himself, if Macbeth "played'st most foully." (3.1.3) This suggests that Banquo feels that Macbeth became king as a result of regicide. Despite this, Banquo still hopes that the Witches' prophecy that he will be the "father of many kings" (3.1.5-6) will come true, showing that Banquo cannot fully dismiss the Witches. This perhaps reflects the contradictory relationship many in Shakespeare's time would have had with the supernatural; they believed in Protestant Christianity, which rejected the perceived 'superstition' of Roman Catholicism, whilst simultaneously fearing omens and persecuting 'witches.'

By the end, Shakespeare presents Macbeth as having full confidence in the supernatural which seems now to have taken complete control of the plot of the play. Macbeth revisits the Witches who give him, he believes, good news: "no man of woman born shall harm Macbeth." (4.1.79-80) They add that Macbeth cannot be harmed until Birnham Wood move to Dunsinane. Macbeth seems relieved as these apparent impossibilities, he believes, mean he cannot be killed. Macbeth has clearly fallen completely under the Witches' persuasive spell which is presented through grotesque spectacle and other-worldly trochaic rhythm. The audience, having heard the Witches planning "double, double toil and trouble" (4.1.10) know that they are not to be trusted and this proves to be true as Act 5 plays out and Macbeth reaches a moment of realisation, a feature common to many tragic heroes, that he has been duped by the supernatural and life is merely "a tale...signifying nothing." (5.5.25-27) This suggests that Macbeth has lost faith in everything, including any vestiges of Christian belief - bleak nihilism is his only resort. The contrast to the pious King Edward (3.6.27), who believes most earnestly in approved Christian supernatural beliefs rather than the illegitimate supernatural beliefs that Macbeth professes, would have been very striking to the original, largely Christian, audience.

Thus, in *Macbeth*, Shakespeare presents Banquo and Macbeth's attitudes to the supernatural initially differing and subsequently changing over the course of the drama. Banquo is a voice of reason, dismissing the Witches and counselling caution but later he cannot resist being excited by their prophecy. Macbeth is won over almost immediately believes the Witches with very little questioning. By the end of the play, however, Macbeth's inability to interpret the Witches correctly leads him to believe in his own invincibility. His credulity renders him foolish, and he dies a traitor's death.

2: Essay Writing Checklist

As you read, check how many of the recommendations below are followed by the essay. Then, use the checklist to help you write your own essay.

Remember that these are *recommendations* from an experienced teacher, not *requirements*. Allow them to help and guide you, but don't allow them to restrict you; if you have a different idea and feel confident about it, then give it a go!

- ☐ Use wording of question in answer – "Shakespeare presents."
- ☐ Use Intro and Conclusion to help structure essay as argument.
- ☐ Use topic sentences to open each main paragraph.
- ☐ Close focus on extract.
- ☐ Focus on elsewhere in the play.
- ☐ Use short, precise quotations to support interpretations.
- ☐ Close analysis of language, especially aspects of poetry.
- ☐ Close analysis of form, especially aspects of performance.
- ☐ Close analysis of text structure, especially aspects of tragedy.
- ☐ Refer to effect on audience.
- ☐ Use relevant subject terminology.
- ☐ Connect to context when text was written, where relevant: Jacobean era.
- ☐ Connect to context when text is set, where relevant: early medieval Scotland.
- ☐ Connect to literary context, where relevant: history of the genre of tragedy.
- ☐ Connect to original and 21st century audience context, where relevant.
- ☐ Focus on minor character(s), where relevant.
- ☐ Use accurate spelling, punctuation and grammar.
- ☐ Write c450-c750 words.

3: A violent character

Read the following extract from Act 1 Scene 2 of *Macbeth* and then answer the question that follows.

At this point in the play, the Captain tells Duncan about Macbeth's part in the recent battle.

CAPTAIN

Doubtful it stood,
As two spent swimmers that do cling together
And choke their art. The merciless Macdonald –
Worthy to be a rebel, for to that
The multiplying villainies of nature
Do swarm upon him – from the Western Isles
Of kerns and galloglasses is supplied,
And Fortune on his damned quarrel smiling,
Show'd like a rebel's whore. But all's too weak,
For brave Macbeth – well he deserves that name –
Disdaining Fortune, with his brandish'd steel,
Which smok'd with bloody execution,
Like Valour's minion carv'd out his passage
Till he fac'd the slave,
Which ne'er shook hands, nor bade farewell to him,
Till he unseam'd him from the nave to th'chaps
And fix'd his head upon our battlements.

Starting with this speech, explore how Shakespeare presents Macbeth as a violent character.

Write about:

- how Shakespeare presents Macbeth in this extract
- how Shakespeare presents Macbeth as a violent character in the play as a whole.

3: The Essay

Shakespeare presents Macbeth as an incredibly violent character. In the extract, the Captain celebrates Macbeth's violent quashing of a rebellion against King Duncan. Later, we see Macbeth initially unwilling to be violent; however, he then relents and kills Duncan. After becoming king, Macbeth delegates violence to hired murderers and is responsible for a series of killings. Finally, Macbeth's tyranny provokes an invasion and Macbeth meets his deserved end, violently. Shakespeare shows that Macbeth's violence in defence of Scotland is celebrated but his violence for his own, illegitimate, ends is condemned.

In the extract, Shakespeare shows how the Captain celebrates Macbeth's violence, creating a favourable impression of the Thane of Glamis before his first appearance on stage. The Captain condemns Macdonald as being "like a rebel's whore." (1.2.15) This insulting simile emphasises how immoral Macdonald is and heightens the contrast with virtuous Macbeth. The Captain then praises Macbeth, portraying him as winning the battle single-handedly, recounting that his sword "smok'd with bloody execution." (1.2.18) These metaphors combine liquid blood and burning fire to suggest that the blood of the rebels seemed to burn on Macbeth's sword. The final moment is gory and disgusting as Macbeth "unseam'd" Macdonald "from the nave to th'chaps." (1.2.22) Again, the Captain emphasises Macbeth's strength and also seeks to present Macdonald in the worst light as this death is shameful and ridiculous – a traitor's death. It is clear that for the Captain and his royal audience, and indeed Shakespeare's audience in The Globe, Macbeth's violence is to be applauded as it was done in defence of his nation and his legitimate monarch.

Later, Shakespeare presents Macbeth using violence to fulfil his ambition. Macbeth is initially reluctant to kill Duncan and only the angry mockery of his wife, who sees his reluctance as un-masculine weakness, persuades him to "do all that may become a man." (1.7.46) This shows that Lady Macbeth's mockery has worked; Macbeth clearly reacts against being seen as effeminate. Moments after killing the king, Macbeth tells us he was unable to join the grooms in earnest prayer: "I could not say 'Amen'." (2.2.31) This suggests that, knowing how sinful regicide is, Macbeth is already distancing himself from the possibility of forgiveness and redemption offered by Christian belief. After killing Duncan, Macbeth wrestles with his guilt and desperately tries to wash the blood away, wondering if "all great Neptune's ocean" (2.2.63) might be needed. This hyperbole emphasises how Macbeth fears that the stain of his sin will be on his soul forever. In fact, in an era of belief in the Divine Right of Kings, many in Shakespeare's original audience would have believed that murder of a monarch is tantamount to murder of God, the worst sin imaginable.

Elsewhere in the play, Shakespeare presents Macbeth as a tyrant who embroils all around him in his violence. Macbeth employs murderers and then commands night's "bloody and invisible hand" (3.3.48) and "black agents" (3.3.53) to kill Banquo and Fleance. This personification and commanding of night, an echo perhaps of Lady Macbeth's similar commanding of night (1.5.49), shows how Macbeth requires supernatural aid, as well as paid murderers, to commit his immoral deeds. Later, Macbeth uses murderers to massacre everyone in Macduff's castle. Macduff's anguished cries when he learns of the deaths of "all [his] pretty chickens and their dam," (4.3.220) create a shocking juxtaposition between Macduff's pet names for his family and the audience's recent witnessing of their brutal deaths, crystallising how far Macbeth has changed from loyal soldier to violent child killer. Before his death, Macbeth reveals in a soliloquy his realisation of the full extent of this change. He notices that a "night-shriek" (5.5.11) does not affect him because he has "supp'd full with horrors." (5.5.13) The metaphor suggests that Macbeth has feasted on violence and another forkful of horror signifies nothing to him now. He proves this moments later as, on being informed the shriek marks the death of Lady Macbeth, his response is to ruminate nihilistically on the pointlessness of life rather than mourn his wife.

Thus, Shakespeare does indeed present Macbeth as a violent character, highlighting a debate that still resonates: can violence ever be legitimate? It is clear that for Macbeth's contemporaries, his violence as a soldier is valiant, brave and befitting of a man. His later violent acts are presented as increasingly immoral, the products of a sick mind. Ultimately, an invading army is required to topple Macbeth. Shakespeare perhaps suggests in *Macbeth* that violence begets violence and that without the "grace of Grace" (5.9.39), the vicious cycle will continue.

3: Essay Writing Checklist

As you read, check how many of the recommendations below are followed by the essay. Then, use the checklist to help you write your own essay.

Remember that these are *recommendations* from an experienced teacher, not *requirements*. Allow them to help and guide you, but don't allow them to restrict you; if you have a different idea and feel confident about it, then give it a go!

- ☐ Use wording of question in answer – "Shakespeare presents."
- ☐ Use Intro and Conclusion to help structure essay as argument.
- ☐ Use topic sentences to open each main paragraph.
- ☐ Close focus on extract.
- ☐ Focus on elsewhere in the play.
- ☐ Use short, precise quotations to support interpretations.
- ☐ Close analysis of language, especially aspects of poetry.
- ☐ Close analysis of form, especially aspects of performance.
- ☐ Close analysis of text structure, especially aspects of tragedy.
- ☐ Refer to effect on audience.
- ☐ Use relevant subject terminology.
- ☐ Connect to context when text was written, where relevant: Jacobean era.
- ☐ Connect to context when text is set, where relevant: early medieval Scotland.
- ☐ Connect to literary context, where relevant: history of the genre of tragedy.
- ☐ Connect to original and 21st century audience context, where relevant.
- ☐ Focus on minor character(s), where relevant.
- ☐ Use accurate spelling, punctuation and grammar.
- ☐ Write c450-c750 words.

4: A changing female character

Read the following extract from Act 5 Scene 1 of Macbeth and then answer the question that follows.

At this point in the play, the Doctor and the Gentlewoman watch Lady Macbeth sleepwalking.

LADY MACBETH Out, damned spot! Out, I say! One, two. Why then 'tis time to do't. Hell is murky. Fie, my lord, fie, a soldier, and afeard? What need we fear who knows it, when none can call our power to account? Yet who would have thought the old man to have had so much blood in him?

DOCTOR Do you mark that?

LADY MACBETH The Thane of Fife had a wife. Where is she now? What, will these hands ne'er be clean? No more o'that, my Lord, no more o'that. You mar all with this starting.

DOCTOR Go to, go to; you have known what you should not.

GENTLEWOMAN She has spoke what she should not, I am sure of that. Heaven knows what she has known.

LADY MACBETH Here's the smell of the blood still; all the perfumes of Arabia will not sweeten this little hand. O, O, O.

DOCTOR What a sigh is there! The heart is sorely charged.

GENTLEWOMAN I would not have such a heart in my bosom for the dignity of the whole body.

DOCTOR Well, well, well –

GENTLEWOMAN Pray God it be, sir.

DOCTOR This disease is beyond my practice; yet I have known those which have walked in their sleep who have died holily in their beds.

LADY MACBETH Wash your hands, put on your night-gown, look not so pale. I tell you yet again, Banquo's buried; he cannot come out on's grave.

DOCTOR Even so?

LADY MACBETH To bed, to bed; there's knocking at the gate. Come, come, come, come, give me your hand; what's done cannot be undone. To bed, to bed, to bed.

'Lady Macbeth is a female character who changes during the play.'

Starting with this moment in the play, explore how far you agree with this view.

Write about:

- how Shakespeare presents Lady Macbeth in this extract
- how far Shakespeare presents Lady Macbeth as a female character who changes in the play as a whole.

4: The Essay

Lady Macbeth is indeed presented as a changing female character in *Macbeth*. In Act One, she is a determined woman, the driving force behind the plot to kill Duncan. Later, however, her husband rejects her advice, and she largely disappears from the story. When we see her again, she is a different, weaker character, shuffling around the stage, attacked by her conscience. Shakespeare crafts a compelling character who dramatically transgresses the stereotypes of her era, then changes utterly and is ultimately destroyed.

In the extract, Shakespeare shows that Lady Macbeth has changed since the banquet. She sleepwalks, revealing shocking clues about the murder of King Duncan, wondering that he had "so much blood." (5.1.35-36) Speaking in disjointed prose, her mind flitting from idea to idea, she presents a stark contrast to her previous strength and poise and suggests that she is psychologically disturbed by her guilty conscience. As she sleepwalks, she compulsively rubs her hands. She apparently believes them to be covered in blood and declares that no amount of "all the perfumes of Arabia" (5.1.44-45) would sufficiently cleanse her, neither of the blood nor of her sin. The blood imagery and the hyperbole show how far Lady Macbeth's previous cruel indifference has changed into guilt and fear. Then, Lady Macbeth prepares for bed declaring that "what's done cannot be undone." (5.1.59-60) This is the last time we see her, and her behaviour perhaps suggests she has reached a state of acceptance and is ready for death, and for hell. Thus, Shakespeare shows that, eaten away by her guilty conscience, Lady Macbeth is sent mad and driven her to commit one last act considered sinful by many in the era: suicide.

Earlier in the play, however, Shakespeare presents Lady Macbeth as a strong, determined woman. She calls on spirits to "unsex" (1.5.40) her and "take [her] milk for gall." (1.5.47) This suggests that she will not allow any nurturing instinct to stop her. Instead, she commands the spirts to fill her full "of direst cruelty" (1.5.42) and suppress "compunctious visitings of nature" (1.5.44) from causing her to feel remorse. This shocking imagery suggests that she seeks to be pure, uncaring evil in order to be an accomplice to regicide. Then, Lady Macbeth is presented as an active participant in the crime, planting the daggers on Duncan's grooms. Returning to the stage, she sneers at Macbeth's terrified response to his bloody hands, declaring that "a little water clears us of the deed." (2.2.70) This shows that she mocks her husband's guilt, before changing, late in the play and echoing Macbeth's desperate handwashing, as a sign of her delayed guilt. This depiction of female control in a marriage would have been surprising to the original audience who may have expected Macbeth to be in control and shows that Lady Macbeth is presented as transgressing the stereotypes of the era.

In Act Three, Shakespeare presents how Lady Macbeth capably plays her role as a powerful monarch, continuing to support and influence her husband, but increasingly side-lined by him. Before the banquet, she advises Macbeth to be "bright and jovial." (3.2.28) She shows how concerned she is by Macbeth's mental state, suggesting that she knows that they must appear regal and strong in order to have a chance of retaining the loyalty of the thanes. Macbeth dismisses Lady Macbeth's concerns, waving her away with the diminutive "chuck." (3.2.45) This shows that Macbeth is decreasingly reliant on Lady Macbeth and signals the beginning of her isolation. At the banquet, Lady Macbeth sits alone on her throne, visibly at the height of her power but she struggles to regain control when Macbeth breaks down, publicly commanding the thanes with a series of imperatives and privately berating Macbeth for his actions more suited for a "woman's story at a winter's fire." (3.4.65) Here, Lady Macbeth is presented as still having some control, echoing her earlier mockery of Macbeth's lack of manliness, but it is too late; this is the last time we see her before her incredible transformation into the guilt-ridden sleepwalker of Act Five.

Thus, Shakespeare does indeed present Lady Macbeth as a female character who changes radically during the play. Through clear strategic thinking and filled with evil by supernatural spirits, she fulfils her ambition to be queen. For a moment, sitting alone on a throne, deferred to by the most powerful men in Scotland, she is at the height of her prestige. However, her downfall is quick and spectacular. Wracked by late-arriving guilt, suicide is her only escape, thereby condemning her, in the eyes of the Early Modern Christian audience, to eternal punishment in hell.

4: Essay Writing Checklist

As you read, check how many of the recommendations below are followed by the essay. Then, use the checklist to help you write your own essay.

Remember that these are *recommendations* from an experienced teacher, not *requirements*. Allow them to help and guide you, but don't allow them to restrict you; if you have a different idea and feel confident about it, then give it a go!

- ☐ Use wording of question in answer – "Shakespeare presents."
- ☐ Use Intro and Conclusion to help structure essay as argument.
- ☐ Use topic sentences to open each main paragraph.
- ☐ Close focus on extract.
- ☐ Focus on elsewhere in the play.
- ☐ Use short, precise quotations to support interpretations.
- ☐ Close analysis of language, especially aspects of poetry.
- ☐ Close analysis of form, especially aspects of performance.
- ☐ Close analysis of text structure, especially aspects of tragedy.
- ☐ Refer to effect on audience.
- ☐ Use relevant subject terminology.
- ☐ Connect to context when text was written, where relevant: Jacobean era.
- ☐ Connect to context when text is set, where relevant: early medieval Scotland.
- ☐ Connect to literary context, where relevant: history of the genre of tragedy.
- ☐ Connect to original and 21st century audience context, where relevant.
- ☐ Focus on minor character(s), where relevant.
- ☐ Use accurate spelling, punctuation and grammar.
- ☐ Write c450-c750 words.

5: A powerful woman

Read the following extract from Act 1 Scene 5 of *Macbeth* and then answer the question that follows.

At this point in the play Lady Macbeth is speaking. She has just received the news that King Duncan will be spending the night at her castle.

LADY MACBETH
The raven himself is hoarse
That croaks the fatal entrance of Duncan
Under my battlements. Come, you spirits
That tend on mortal thoughts, unsex me here,
And fill me from the crown to the toe topfull
Of direst cruelty; make thick my blood,
Stop up th'access and passage to remorse
That no compunctious visitings of nature
Shake my fell purpose nor keep peace between
Th'effect and it. Come to my woman's breasts,
And take my milk for gall, you murd'ring ministers,
Wherever in your sightless substances
You wait on nature's mischief. Come, thick night,
And pall thee in the dunnest smoke of hell,
That my keen knife see not the wound it makes
Nor heaven peep through the blanket of the dark,
To cry 'Hold, hold!'

Starting with this speech, explain how far you think Shakespeare presents Lady Macbeth as a powerful woman.

Write about:

- how Shakespeare presents Lady Macbeth in this speech
- how Shakespeare presents Lady Macbeth in the play as a whole.

5: The Essay

Shakespeare presents Lady Macbeth, early in the play, as an ambitious aristocrat, desperate for more power and willing to use the terrible forces of the supernatural get it. She commands her husband, transgressing contemporary expectations of a wife's behaviour. As queen, she commands, and is deferred to by, the most powerful men of Scotland. However, by the end of the play, Shakespeare presents Lady Macbeth as powerless, tormented by guilt and ignored by her husband. With her suicide, Shakespeare perhaps suggests that her hunger for power was illegitimate and deserving of the eternal punishment of hell.

In the extract, Shakespeare shows Lady Macbeth commanding supernatural spirits to help her to increase her power. She reveals her private thoughts in a soliloquy, calling on the spirits to "unsex" (1.5.40) her and fill her with cruelty. This suggests that she feels being a woman is an impediment to taking such an extreme step and she needs supernatural aid to become sufficiently remorseless. She continues to shed aspects of her femininity, commanding the spirits to "take my milk for gall." (1.5.47) The imagery of nurturing milk being replaced with bitter poison shows that Lady Macbeth is so desperate for power that she is willing to become something inhuman, un-natural. She then calls on the night to "pall thee in the dunnest smoke of hell" (1.5.50) so that heaven cannot see the crime she plans to commit. This imagery shows that she is willing to sin to fulfil her ambition. In an era of witch trials and the burning of heretics, Lady Macbeth would have appeared as representative of everything the contemporary audience feared: a woman, refusing to be a stereotypical mother figure, seeking her own power through supernatural means, in open contravention of God's law.

As the play progresses, Shakespeare shows Lady Macbeth gaining power. When Macbeth commands her to abort their murder plot, she declares that she would have "dash'd the brains out" (1.7.54) of her child if she were similarly vacillating. This violent image, along with use of the non-familiar 'you' pronoun, shows how Lady Macbeth is willing to use powerful language to frighten and control Macbeth. It also shows how she continues to reject the role of nurturing mother in favour of the more powerful roles of regicide and queen. Lady Macbeth takes complete control after Macbeth's "brain-sickly" (2.2.49) breakdown, returning to the crime scene to rub blood on the grooms' faces, dismissing Macbeth's remorse as a shameful mental illness. In Act 3, Lady Macbeth sits enthroned alone, visibly at the height of her power but she struggles to regain control when Macbeth again breaks down, publicly commanding the thanes with a series of imperatives and privately berating Macbeth for his actions more suited for a "woman's story at a winter's fire." (3.4.65) She again mocks Macbeth's perceived lack of manliness but her power, reliant on Macbeth, is in jeopardy.

In Act Five, Shakespeare presents Lady Macbeth as weak and powerless. She sleepwalks, revealing clues about King Duncan's death, wondering that he had "so much blood." (5.1.35-36) Speaking in disjointed prose, her mind flitting from idea to idea, she presents a stark contrast to her previous power and poise and suggests that she is psychologically disturbed by her guilty conscience. As she sleepwalks, she compulsively rubs her hands. She apparently believes them to be bloody and declares that no amount of "all the perfumes of Arabia" (5.1.44-45) would sufficiently cleanse her, neither of the blood nor of her sin. The blood imagery and the hyperbole show how far Lady Macbeth's previous powerful defiance ("a little water clears us of this deed" 2.2.70) has changed into guilt and fear. Then, Lady Macbeth exits declaring that "what's done cannot be undone," (5.1.59-60) showing recognition of her powerlessness. This is her last time on stage and her behaviour, and subsequent suicide, suggest she has reached a state of acceptance and is ready for death, and for hell; eaten away by her guilty conscience, Lady Macbeth loses all power and control, even over her own life.

Thus, Shakespeare shows us Lady Macbeth transforming from ambitious aristocrat to a powerful queen. She plans a murder plot, dominates her husband and uses the supernatural to reject what she perceives to be 'feminine' weakness. Her downfall is rapid and shocking. Side-lined by Macbeth she fades into obscurity before succumbing to mental torment and suicide. Many in the original audience would interpret her end as a just punishment for her transgressive, criminal, behaviour; modern adaptations invoke more sympathy for the character, presenting Lady Macbeth as more victim than villain. The drama of Lady Macbeth's character trajectory continues to fascinate and generate new interpretations.

5: Essay Writing Checklist

As you read, check how many of the recommendations below are followed by the essay. Then, use the checklist to help you write your own essay.

Remember that these are *recommendations* from an experienced teacher, not *requirements*. Allow them to help and guide you, but don't allow them to restrict you; if you have a different idea and feel confident about it, then give it a go!

- [ ] Use wording of question in answer – "Shakespeare presents."
- [ ] Use Intro and Conclusion to help structure essay as argument.
- [ ] Use topic sentences to open each main paragraph.
- [ ] Close focus on extract.
- [ ] Focus on elsewhere in the play.
- [ ] Use short, precise quotations to support interpretations.
- [ ] Close analysis of language, especially aspects of poetry.
- [ ] Close analysis of form, especially aspects of performance.
- [ ] Close analysis of text structure, especially aspects of tragedy.
- [ ] Refer to effect on audience.
- [ ] Use relevant subject terminology.
- [ ] Connect to context when text was written, where relevant: Jacobean era.
- [ ] Connect to context when text is set, where relevant: early medieval Scotland.
- [ ] Connect to literary context, where relevant: history of the genre of tragedy.
- [ ] Connect to original and 21st century audience context, where relevant.
- [ ] Focus on minor character(s), where relevant.
- [ ] Use accurate spelling, punctuation and grammar.
- [ ] Write c450-c750 words.

6: A hero

Read the following question from Act 5 Scene 3 of *Macbeth* and then answer the question that follows.

At this point in the play Macbeth is under siege from the English army.

MACBETH
Bring me no more reports; let them fly all:
Till Birnam wood remove to Dunsinane,
I cannot taint with fear. What's the boy Malcolm?
Was he not born of woman? The spirits that know
All mortal consequences have pronounc'd me thus:
'Fear not, Macbeth; no man that's born of woman
Shall e'er have power upon thee.' Then fly, false thanes,
And mingle with the English epicures:
The mind I sway by and the heart I bear
Shall never sag with doubt nor shake with fear.
Enter a Servant
The devil damn thee black, thou cream-fac'd loon!
Where got'st thou that goose look?

Starting with this speech, explain how far you think Shakespeare presents Macbeth as a hero.

Write about:

- how Shakespeare presents Macbeth in this speech
- how Shakespeare presents Macbeth in the play as a whole.

6: The Essay

In *Macbeth*, Shakespeare initially presents the protagonist as a brave military hero. However, Macbeth then performs a series of immoral actions, including murdering Duncan and seizing the throne. By the end of the play, Macbeth's military prowess re-appears as we see him bravely taking on an entire army alone, but these are presented as the actions not of a hero but of a desperate tyrant. Though Macbeth rarely evinces positive heroism, as the protagonist of a tragedy, he can be interpreted as being a tragic hero: a flawed character who undergoes a reversal of fortune.

In the extract, Shakespeare presents Macbeth as a military hero, defiantly preparing for battle. Macbeth finds comfort in the Witches' words, directly quoting them as if to convince himself of their veracity and proclaiming that he cannot "taint with fear." (5.3.3) This suggests that he sees fear as unbefitting of a military hero. It also shows that he believes in his own invincibility. He then contrasts his courage with the disloyal thanes and their soft-living English allies, suggesting that, as he can never "shake with fear," (5.3.10) he is a bold hero compared to them. The audience, however, may not have the same confidence in the Witches' prophecies as Macbeth, leading to dramatic irony as we interpret Macbeth's actions as those of a desperate tyrant rather than those of a hero. This is confirmed when Macbeth is presented attacking the servant, repeatedly, for being pale and, Macbeth infers, scared: "thou cream-faced loon." (5.3.11) This presents Macbeth not as a hero, nor a good leader, but as a tyrannous, angry fool, apparently fixating on his servant's pale face, and disbelieving his message, rather than thinking clearly and acting with bravery as we might expect from a hero.

At the start of the play, Shakespeare first introduces us to Macbeth via the Captain's breathless praise of his heroism. The Captain contrasts the "rebel's whore" (1.2.15) Macdonald with the brave hero Macbeth whose sword "smoked with bloody execution." (1.2.18) This imagery combines liquid blood and burning fire to suggest that the blood of the rebels seemed to burn on Macbeth's righteous sword. The Captain recounts how Macbeth and Banquo redouble their efforts and shed much more blood when the battle is renewed as if, he wonders, to "memorize another Golgotha." (1.2.40) The allusion to the Crucifixion perhaps suggests that, for the Captain, Macbeth is a hero, as Jesus is to a Christian audience. However, the audience may struggle to identify Macbeth with Jesus, identifying him instead with the villainy of the Roman soldiers at the foot of the cross. This impression of Macbeth's villainy is confirmed soon after when Macbeth's aside, revealing his "black and deep desires" (1.4.51) shows how, even at the moment he is being celebrated and rewarded for his heroism, he is already considering regicide; Macbeth is no hero.

Later in the play, Shakespeare shows that Macbeth no longer has the traditional attributes of a hero and, instead, is embarked on the downwards trajectory of a tragic hero. Macbeth is presented as irreligious, unable to join the sleeping grooms in prayer: "'Amen' stuck in my throat." (2.2.35-36) A hero would not be so distanced from God nor, indeed, so willing to commit treason and murder. Macbeth then wields his sword against Scotland, cutting a swathe through his own people, not even sparing children who, as "young fry of treachery" (4.2.81) are equally subject to Macbeth's tyranny. Heroes, it is suggested, do not kill kings, nor do they kill children. As the army gathers to depose him, Macduff denounces Macbeth as "an untitl'd tyrant, bloody sceptr'd...fiend of Scotland." (4.3.104 and 236) Noble Macduff, and others in the England camp, including pious King Edward, who have the "powers above" (4.3.241) on their side are contrasted with the detested villain Macbeth. Though Macbeth clearly has none of the positive traits of a hero, by this point of the play, his downfall as a tragic hero is gathering speed as he plummets towards his own personal Golgotha.

Shakespeare, then, presents to his audience the story of a brave warrior, who, dissatisfied by his reward for such heroism seizes power and proceeds to rule Scotland as a tyrant. A litany of immoral, unheroic, crimes follows as Macbeth plummets towards his death. In this way, Macbeth's story follows the traditional arc of the tragic hero but, it could be argued, the true heroes in the text are Macduff and his allies who, unselfishly, act for the best interests of Scotland in deposing Macbeth and placing the rightful monarch on the throne.

6: Essay Writing Checklist

As you read, check how many of the recommendations below are followed by the essay. Then, use the checklist to help you write your own essay.

Remember that these are *recommendations* from an experienced teacher, not *requirements*. Allow them to help and guide you, but don't allow them to restrict you; if you have a different idea and feel confident about it, then give it a go!

- ☐ Use wording of question in answer – "Shakespeare presents."
- ☐ Use Intro and Conclusion to help structure essay as argument.
- ☐ Use topic sentences to open each main paragraph.
- ☐ Close focus on extract.
- ☐ Focus on elsewhere in the play.
- ☐ Use short, precise quotations to support interpretations.
- ☐ Close analysis of language, especially aspects of poetry.
- ☐ Close analysis of form, especially aspects of performance.
- ☐ Close analysis of text structure, especially aspects of tragedy.
- ☐ Refer to effect on audience.
- ☐ Use relevant subject terminology.
- ☐ Connect to context when text was written, where relevant: Jacobean era.
- ☐ Connect to context when text is set, where relevant: early medieval Scotland.
- ☐ Connect to literary context, where relevant: history of the genre of tragedy.
- ☐ Connect to original and 21st century audience context, where relevant.
- ☐ Focus on minor character(s), where relevant.
- ☐ Use accurate spelling, punctuation and grammar.
- ☐ Write c450-c750 words.

7: Marriage

Read the following extract from Act 1 Scene 7 of *Macbeth* and then answer the question that follows.

At this moment in the play, Macbeth has left the banquet he and his wife are holding for Duncan, and his wife has come to find him.

LADY MACBETH
He has almost supp'd. Why have you left the chamber?
MACBETH
Hath he ask'd for me?
LADY MACBETH
Know you not, he has?
MACBETH
We will proceed no further in this business.
He hath honour'd me of late, and I have bought
Golden opinions from all sorts of people,
Which would be worn now in their newest gloss,
Not cast aside so soon.
LADY MACBETH
Was the hope drunk
Wherein you dress'd yourself? Hath it slept since?
And wakes it now to look so green and pale
At what it did so freely? From this time,
Such I account thy love. Art thou afeard
To be the same in thine own act and valour,
As thou art in desire? Wouldst thou have that
Which thou esteem'st the ornament of life,
And live a coward in thine own esteem,
Letting I dare not wait upon I would,
Like the poor cat i'th'adage?
MACBETH
Prithee, peace.
I dare do all that may become a man;
Who dares do more is none.

Starting with this moment in the play, explore how Shakespeare presents the marriage between Macbeth and Lady Macbeth.

Write about:

- how Shakespeare presents their relationship at this moment in the play
- how Shakespeare presents their marriage in the play as a whole.

7: The Essay

In *Macbeth*, Shakespeare presents the Macbeths' marriage as central to the plot of the tragedy. The closeness of their relationship is demonstrated early in the play as they conspire together to fulfil their shared ambition. Shakespeare also shows that Lady Macbeth flouts conventional ideas about marital roles; she seeks to control her husband, using mockery and anger to manipulate him. However, their relationship becomes strained as Macbeth descends increasingly into tyranny and murder and, by the end of the play, their marriage appears to have broken down and Lady Macbeth dies alone and un-mourned.

In the extract, Shakespeare presents the Macbeths' relationship as close yet turbulent. In a private conversation, Macbeth commands Lady Macbeth to "proceed no further" (1.7.31) in their murder plot. His imperative tone suggests that he expects to be obeyed. However, Lady Macbeth rapidly takes control with a barrage of questions that Macbeth is given no space to answer. She mockingly suggests he will be a foolish "coward," (1.7.43) "like the poor cat i'th'adage," (1.7.45) who wants to eat fish but won't get her feet wet. This shows that it is Lady Macbeth, in fact, who dominates and will not allow Macbeth to destroy her dreams. It also shows that she knows what motivates Macbeth, which is made clear by his reaction. He bristles and states, rather unconvincingly, that he will "dare do all that may become a man." (1.7.46) Macbeth feels that his masculinity is under question and, rather than be deemed an effeminate coward, will proceed with the plot. Lady Macbeth, flouting traditional conventions of the meek and passive wife, has won the argument and will soon be queen.

In Act Three, Shakespeare presents the Macbeths' relationship as beginning to fracture. Before the banquet, again in a private conversation signalling their closeness, Lady Macbeth advises Macbeth to be "bright and jovial" (3.2.28) She shows how concerned she is by Macbeth's mental state, suggesting that she has doubts about his ability to conceal their subterfuge. Macbeth dismisses her concerns with the diminutive "chuck" (3.2.45), choosing not to involve her in his new murder plots. This is in stark contrast to his previous deference to her and their earlier bond of trust, showing that Macbeth is decreasingly reliant on Lady Macbeth. This moment also reverses the relative status of the two characters so that their marriage now seems more conventional. At the banquet, when Macbeth breaks down, Lady Macbeth publicly commands the thanes with a series of imperatives and privately berates Macbeth for his actions more suited for a "woman's story at a winter's fire." (3.4.65) Here, Lady Macbeth regains some of her previous dominance, echoing her earlier mockery of Macbeth's lack of manliness, but it is too late; this is the last time we see her before her incredible transformation into the guilt-ridden solitary sleepwalker of Act Five.

By the end of the play, Shakespeare shows that the Macbeths' marriage has completely broken down. Lady Macbeth sleepwalks, questioning and mocking Macbeth: "fie, my lord, fie a soldier, and afeard?" (5.1.32-33) Calling him her lord, and his absence from stage, shows again how her status in their marriage has fallen but her mockery suggests she still has no faith in Macbeth. She refers to the only other married couple seen in the play, wondering of Lady Macduff, "where is she now?" (5.1.38) Perhaps she suspects that Lady Macduff and her children have been murdered. The contrast between the loving, fruitful, conventional marriage of the Macduffs and the murderous, sterile, unconventional marriage of the Macbeths is striking and emphasises how far their marriage has failed. When Macbeth hears of his wife's suicide, rather than expressing grief, similar to how Macduff reacted on hearing of his family's murder, Macbeth instead ruminates on the emptiness of life which, he now believes, is "a tale told by an idiot...signifying nothing." (5.5.25-27) This shows how completely their marriage has broken down. Once it bound them together in a plan to seize the throne; now it has torn them apart and they both die, un-loved and un-mourned.

Thus, Shakespeare shows that the Macbeths' marriage is the opposite of everything the audience may hope a marriage could be. The initial closeness of Macbeth and Lady Macbeth hints at love and trust that they maybe shared once but the events of the play show that that love and trust died long ago, transforming instead into mockery, anger and manipulation. Ultimately, though demonstrating unconventional dominance early in the play, Lady Macbeth is rejected by Macbeth once she is no longer useful to him, as he asserts his tyranny over her and over the people of Scotland.

7: Essay Writing Checklist

As you read, check how many of the recommendations below are followed by the essay. Then, use the checklist to help you write your own essay.

Remember that these are *recommendations* from an experienced teacher, not *requirements*. Allow them to help and guide you, but don't allow them to restrict you; if you have a different idea and feel confident about it, then give it a go!

- ☐ Use wording of question in answer – "Shakespeare presents."
- ☐ Use Intro and Conclusion to help structure essay as argument.
- ☐ Use topic sentences to open each main paragraph.
- ☐ Close focus on extract.
- ☐ Focus on elsewhere in the play.
- ☐ Use short, precise quotations to support interpretations.
- ☐ Close analysis of language, especially aspects of poetry.
- ☐ Close analysis of form, especially aspects of performance.
- ☐ Close analysis of text structure, especially aspects of tragedy.
- ☐ Refer to effect on audience.
- ☐ Use relevant subject terminology.
- ☐ Connect to context when text was written, where relevant: Jacobean era.
- ☐ Connect to context when text is set, where relevant: early medieval Scotland.
- ☐ Connect to literary context, where relevant: history of the genre of tragedy.
- ☐ Connect to original and 21st century audience context, where relevant.
- ☐ Focus on minor character(s), where relevant.
- ☐ Use accurate spelling, punctuation and grammar.
- ☐ Write c450-c750 words.

8: The Macduffs

Read the following extract from Act 4 Scene 3 of *Macbeth* and then answer the question that follows.

At this moment in the play, Macduff has just been told of the murder of his wife and children.

MALCOLM
Dispute it like a man.
MACDUFF
I shall do so;
But I must also feel it as a man;
I cannot but remember such things were
That were most precious to me. Did heaven look on,
And would not take their part? Sinful Macduff,
They were all struck for thee. Naught that I am,
Not for their own demerits but for mine,
Fell slaughter on their souls. Heaven rest them now.
MALCOLM
Be this the whetstone of your sword, let grief
Convert to anger. Blunt not the heart, enrage it.
MACDUFF
O, I could play the woman with mine eyes
And braggart with my tongue. But, gentle heavens,
Cut short all intermission. Front to front
Bring thou this fiend of Scotland and myself;
Within my sword's length set him. If he scape,
Heaven forgive him too.

Starting with this moment in the play, explore how Shakespeare presents Macduff and his family in *Macbeth*.

Write about:

- how Shakespeare presents Macduff and his family at this moment in the play
- how Shakespeare presents Macduff and his family in the play as a whole.

8: The Essay

Shakespeare presents the Macduffs as striking contrasts to the Macbeths. While the Macbeths destroy Scotland, Macduff seeks what is best for his nation. The Macbeths are childless and loveless while the Macduff family is loving and happy. Ultimately, Macduff is presented as Macbeth's nemesis, the only man able to kill Macbeth. Embodying love of family, nation and God, Macduff is rewarded for his loyalty by the new king. Shakespeare presents Macduff and his family as role models, suggesting, in a time of dynastic change, that loyalty and morality are more virtuous than greed and ambition.

In the extract, Shakespeare shows Macduff responding to the news of his family's death. Macduff acknowledges that his "demerits" (4.3.229) are the reason why they were killed but at the same time, clearly distressed, he cries out in anger to heaven before praying for the repose of his family's souls. This shows the turbulent wave of emotion Macduff is battling, suggesting he is a genuine, loving character. His emotion continues and he almost weeps: "O, I could play the woman with mine eyes." (4.3.233) However, he holds back his tears, perhaps unwilling to appear weak before his leader, Malcolm, who has already told him to take the news "like a man." (4.3.222) Just as Lady Macbeth does, Malcolm and Macduff clearly associate femininity with weakness. Instead, encouraged by Malcolm to use the grief to whet his desire for revenge, Macduff declares himself ready to face the "fiend of Scotland...within my sword's length." (4.3.236-237) Here Macduff shows steely resolve and his clear awareness of good and evil. Unlike Macbeth who is consumed by his turbulent emotion, Shakespeare presents Macduff as using his anger and grief to drive him to heroic action.

Earlier in the play, Shakespeare presents the Macduffs as honest, caring people. Macduff reacts with horror when he discovers the murder that "broke ope the Lord's anointed temple." (2.3.63-64) His grief appears genuine, especially when compared to Macbeth's obvious dissembling, and his religious language shows that he sees Duncan as God's representative on Earth, an echo perhaps of the Jacobean concept of the Divine Right of Kings. Macduff's suspicions develop, and his response to Macbeth's messenger, "Sir, not I," (3.6.41) shows that he is not afraid to insult Macbeth with his defiant refusal to attend the royal banquet. Back home, Lady Macduff and her son 'prattle' in jovial tones about their situation, reduced now to living "as birds do." (4.2.32) The son's optimistic attitude contrasts horribly with the audience's understanding of the danger he is in as dramatic irony means we have witnessed, in the previous scene, Macbeth's decision to murder Macduff. Lady Macduff's mournful summary of the paradox of the times – "to do harm is often laudable, to do good sometime accounted dangerous folly" (4.2.72-75) – is closer to the truth of their predicament and, shortly after, they are dead. Shakespeare shows that the Macduffs pay dearly for their preference for doing good.

In the final scenes of the play, Shakespeare shows how Macduff's loyalty to his family and to his nation drive him to become Macbeth's nemesis. Macduff rushes ahead of the army, afraid that if Macbeth be killed "with no stroke of mine, my wife and children's ghosts will haunt me still." (5.7.16-17) For Macduff, then, this is a personal mission to avenge his family's deaths. When he confronts Macbeth, Macbeth refuses to fight and Macduff, sneering at his pusillanimity, suggests he my live as "the show and gaze o'th'time," (5.8.24) demonstrating to all and sundry, "'here may you see the tyrant.'" (5.8.27) This shows that Macduff feels that the important moral lesson of the fall of Macbeth needs to be widely broadcast. Moreover, his seven-times use of "tyrant/tyranny" with its connotations of despotic usurper, shows that Macduff sees Macbeth as an illegitimate dictator. Macduff subsequently does indeed make Macbeth a spectacle, displaying "th'usurper's cursed head" (5.9.22) and proclaiming with joy, "the time is free." (5.9.22) This suggests that Macduff feels that Macbeth's death has brought freedom to Scotland. Shakespeare shows, therefore, that Macduff has punished Macbeth's hubris and restored order and peace.

Thus, Shakespeare presents Macduff and his family as good honest people who contrast dramatically with the evil dishonest Macbeths. Though minor characters early in the play, it is Macduff's fate to be Macbeth's killer as Shakespeare shows that he was destined from his caesarean birth to fulfil the Witches' prophecies. Though driven by loyalty to Malcolm and by love of his nation, it is his love for his family drives him to kill the tyrant and shows that, at least sometimes, doing good can be laudable.

8: Essay Writing Checklist

As you read, check how many of the recommendations below are followed by the essay. Then, use the checklist to help you write your own essay.

Remember that these are *recommendations* from an experienced teacher, not *requirements*. Allow them to help and guide you, but don't allow them to restrict you; if you have a different idea and feel confident about it, then give it a go!

- ☐ Use wording of question in answer – "Shakespeare presents."
- ☐ Use Intro and Conclusion to help structure essay as argument.
- ☐ Use topic sentences to open each main paragraph.
- ☐ Close focus on extract.
- ☐ Focus on elsewhere in the play.
- ☐ Use short, precise quotations to support interpretations.
- ☐ Close analysis of language, especially aspects of poetry.
- ☐ Close analysis of form, especially aspects of performance.
- ☐ Close analysis of text structure, especially aspects of tragedy.
- ☐ Refer to effect on audience.
- ☐ Use relevant subject terminology.
- ☐ Connect to context when text was written, where relevant: Jacobean era.
- ☐ Connect to context when text is set, where relevant: early medieval Scotland.
- ☐ Connect to literary context, where relevant: history of the genre of tragedy.
- ☐ Connect to original and 21st century audience context, where relevant.
- ☐ Focus on minor character(s), where relevant.
- ☐ Use accurate spelling, punctuation and grammar.
- ☐ Write c450-c750 words.

9: Appearances and reality

Read the following extract from Act 2 Scene 1 of *Macbeth* and then answer the question that follows.

At this moment in the play, Macbeth is preparing to murder Duncan.

MACBETH
Is this a dagger which I see before me,
The handle toward my hand? Come, let me clutch thee.
I have thee not, and yet I see thee still.
Art thou not, fatal vision, sensible
To feeling as to sight? Or art thou but
A dagger of the mind, a false creation,
Proceeding from the heat-oppressed brain?
I see thee yet, in form as palpable
As this which now I draw.
Thou marshall'st me the way that I was going,
And such an instrument I was to use.
Mine eyes are made the fools o'th'other senses,
Or else worth all the rest. I see thee still,
And on thy blade and dudgeon gouts of blood,
Which was not so before. There's no such thing:
It is the bloody business which informs
Thus to mine eyes. Now o'er the one half-world
Nature seems dead, and wicked dreams abuse
The curtain'd sleep. Witchcraft celebrates
Pale Hecate's off'rings, and wither'd murder,
Alarum'd by his sentinel, the wolf,
Whose howl's his watch, thus with his stealthy pace,
With Tarquin's ravishing strides, towards his design
Moves like a ghost.

'Nothing in *Macbeth* is what it seems. It is hard to understand what is real and what is not.'

Starting with this moment in the play, explore how far you agree with this view.

Write about:

- how Shakespeare presents ideas about appearances and reality in this extract
- how far Shakespeare presents ideas about appearances and reality in the play as a whole.

9: The Essay

In *Macbeth*, Shakespeare does indeed create a world where nothing is what it seems; this is a world in which characters are driven to evil and madness as they spiral into unreality, acting on witches' prophecies, lying to friends and communing with evil spirits. The vision of a dagger, the appearance of Banquo's ghost and Lady Macbeth's sleepwalking all serve to show how far the protagonists lose touch with reality and are engulfed by uncertainty before reality and order return at the point of a sword in the final moments of the play.

In the extract, Shakespeare shows Macbeth vacillating between believing in and rejecting the world of the supernatural. The dagger causes him to wonder if in fact it is a hallucination caused by a "heat-oppressed brain?" (2.1.39) Macbeth seems aware enough of his mental frailties to distrust the vision, rejecting it as a sign of his mental breakdown. The original audience, watching in an era without modern special effects, would have seen an actor grasping at thin air in daylight, emphasising that he is a ridiculous figure. Subsequently, Macbeth wonders aloud if his sight is in fact heightened and "worth all the rest" (2.1.45) of his senses. This suggests that Macbeth believes he is developing a supernatural ability to see beyond reality. The audience may instead feel that Macbeth is being fooled. Then, Macbeth ruminates on the world of night in which "witchcraft celebrates pale Hecate's off'rings." (2.1.51-52) It seems that Macbeth has crossed from the world of reality into the unreal world of the supernatural, seeing himself as one with the witches and ghosts of the night. This boundary now crossed, Duncan is doomed.

Later in the play, Shakespeare shows how Macbeth creates an appearance of majesty and hospitality whilst, in fact, being a murderous tyrant. Before the banquet, Lady Macbeth advises Macbeth to be "bright and jovial." (3.2.28) She evidently knows that, in order to consolidate their power, they must perform the role of monarchs, rather than appear as their true selves: scheming murderers who violated their duty of hospitality by killing three guests. Macbeth follows her lead and, speaking in prose, apparently to emphasise his 'man-of-the-people' act, he says he will "play the humble host." (3.4.4-5) This false humility appears calculated to gain the approval of his guests and to hide the truth lurking, literally, in the person of the hired assassins, at the edge of the stage. The appearance of Banquo's ghost shames Macbeth and causes Lady Macbeth to show her two faces to the audience as she publicly commands the thanes with a series of imperatives and privately berates Macbeth for his actions more suited for a "woman's story at a winter's fire." (3.4.65) This shows that Lady Macbeth knows their power is slipping away and fears that, once the thanes see through appearances to the reality of Macbeth's tyranny, a rebellion will surely follow.

Towards the end of the play, Shakespeare shows that both Macbeth and Lady Macbeth have lost their grasp on reality. Lady Macbeth sleepwalks, crying "out, damned spot!" (5.1.31) She sees spots of blood but the audience, including the Doctor and Gentlewoman, can see that her hands are clean. Unlike earlier in the play, when Lady Macbeth blithely washed real blood from her hands, this appearance of blood, her guilt, cannot be washed away. As she continues to speak in disjointed prose, her mind flitting from idea to idea, the shocked Doctor mutters that "unnatural deeds do breed unnatural troubles." (5.1.63-64) The Doctor witnesses Lady Macbeth's "infected mind" (5.1.64) and sees reality; she is guilty, not sick and he diagnoses her need for a priest to impose penance and prepare her for death and judgment. Then, in Act Five, Shakespeare presents Macbeth reaching a moment of nihilistic realisation in a soliloquy ruminating on the unreality of life which, he declares, is a "tale...full of sound and fury signifying nothing." (5.5.25-27) Macbeth's metaphor presents life as a fiction rather than something concrete and real and shows that this tragic hero has completed his journey from greatness to annihilation.

Thus, Shakespeare shows that the Macbeths are initially able to navigate the world of appearances as they lie to protect their new position. However, as they journey deeper into unreality, they both lose the ability to tell reality from appearances, distrusting each other, their friends and the evidence of their turbulent senses. Tormented by visions and manipulated by the Witches, they race towards their destruction. Reality and order are finally restored by Macduff's sword and the assumption of the throne by the legitimate monarch.

9: Essay Writing Checklist

As you read, check how many of the recommendations below are followed by the essay. Then, use the checklist to help you write your own essay.

Remember that these are *recommendations* from an experienced teacher, not *requirements*. Allow them to help and guide you, but don't allow them to restrict you; if you have a different idea and feel confident about it, then give it a go!

- [ ] Use wording of question in answer – "Shakespeare presents."
- [ ] Use Intro and Conclusion to help structure essay as argument.
- [ ] Use topic sentences to open each main paragraph.
- [ ] Close focus on extract.
- [ ] Focus on elsewhere in the play.
- [ ] Use short, precise quotations to support interpretations.
- [ ] Close analysis of language, especially aspects of poetry.
- [ ] Close analysis of form, especially aspects of performance.
- [ ] Close analysis of text structure, especially aspects of tragedy.
- [ ] Refer to effect on audience.
- [ ] Use relevant subject terminology.
- [ ] Connect to context when text was written, where relevant: Jacobean era.
- [ ] Connect to context when text is set, where relevant: early medieval Scotland.
- [ ] Connect to literary context, where relevant: history of the genre of tragedy.
- [ ] Connect to original and 21st century audience context, where relevant.
- [ ] Focus on minor character(s), where relevant.
- [ ] Use accurate spelling, punctuation and grammar.
- [ ] Write c450-c750 words.

10: Good and evil

Read the following extract from Act 1 Scene 5 of *Macbeth* and then answer the question that follows.

At this point in the play Lady Macbeth is speaking. She has just received the news that King Duncan will be spending the night at her castle.

LADY MACBETH
The raven himself is hoarse
That croaks the fatal entrance of Duncan
Under my battlements. Come, you spirits
That tend on mortal thoughts, unsex me here,
And fill me from the crown to the toe topfull
Of direst cruelty; make thick my blood,
Stop up th'access and passage to remorse
That no compunctious visitings of nature
Shake my fell purpose nor keep peace between
Th'effect and it. Come to my woman's breasts,
And take my milk for gall, you murd'ring ministers,
Wherever in your sightless substances
You wait on nature's mischief. Come, thick night,
And pall thee in the dunnest smoke of hell,
That my keen knife see not the wound it makes
Nor heaven peep through the blanket of the dark,
To cry 'Hold, hold!'

Starting with this moment, explore how Shakespeare presents good and evil in *Macbeth*.

Write about:

- how Shakespeare presents good and evil at this moment in the play
- how Shakespeare presents good and evil in the play as a whole.

10: The Essay

In *Macbeth*, Shakespeare shows how good characters can take fateful decisions that send them on the path to violence and evil. Macbeth and Lady Macbeth are high-ranking aristocrats, yet, driven by ambition and greed, and encouraged by supernatural beings, they decide to perpetrate a series of illegal and horrifying acts. Other characters, by contrast, choose the path of good, despite the deadly disadvantages of remaining loyal to lofty ideals of family, nation and God. Ultimately, Shakespeare shows that, though eclipsed for a period, good reasserts itself; Macbeth's severed head and Malcolm's assumption of the throne symbolise the triumph of good over evil.

In the extract, Shakespeare shows Lady Macbeth crossing the boundary between good and evil. She reveals her private thoughts in a soliloquy, calling on the spirits to "unsex" (1.5.40) her and fill her with cruelty. This suggests that she feels being a woman is an impediment to taking such an extreme step and she needs supernatural aid to become sufficiently evil. She continues to shed aspects of her femininity, commanding the spirits to "take my milk for gall." (1.5.47) The imagery of nurturing milk being replaced with bitter poison shows that Lady Macbeth is so desperate for power that she is willing to become something inhuman, unnaturally evil. She then calls on the night to "pall thee in the dunnest smoke of hell" (1.5.50) so that heaven cannot see the crime she plans to commit. This imagery shows that she is willing to sin to fulfil her ambition. In an era of witch trials and the burning of heretics, Lady Macbeth would have appeared as representative of everything the contemporary audience feared: a woman, refusing to be a stereotypical good mother, seeking her own power through evil means, in open contravention of God's law.

Later, Shakespeare shows the dire effects of evil on the protagonists and on Scotland. Moments after killing the king, Macbeth tells us he was unable to join the grooms in earnest prayer: "I could not say 'Amen'." (2.2.31) This shows that Macbeth's decision to sin is driving him away from God, and the possibility of redemption offered by Christian belief. He has turned decisively towards evil. His evil acts unleash chaos in Scotland as the troubled heavens make dark the day and drive nature wild. Macbeth seems energised by this chaos, calling on the "bloody and invisible hand" (3.2.48) of darkness to carry out his "black and deep desires." (1.5.51) The imagery of blood and darkness, and the invocation of supernatural evil beings, emphasises how far evil has suffused both Macbeth and

Scotland. Lady Macduff is grimly aware of this new state of affairs, commenting bleakly that "to do harm is often laudable, to do good sometime accounted dangerous folly." (4.2.72-75) She realises, too late, that evil has Scotland in its grip and attempting to be good puts her and her family in grave danger; shortly after, they are dead.

At the end of the play, Shakespeare shows how evil is vanquished. During preparations for invasion, Macduff and Malcolm explicitly label Macbeth as "damn'd in evils." (4.3.57) They contrast him with King Edward the Confessor whose "sanctity" (4.3.144), they say, allows him to miraculously cure the King's Evil, an inflammatory disease. This allusion to a practice performed by James VI and I, would have been recognised by the original audience, and, in conjunction with James' promotion of the concept of the Divine Right of Kings, clearly presents the legitimate monarch as an agent of God, in battle against the evil represented by Macbeth. By the end of the play, Macbeth comes to the realisation that he has "supp'd full with horrors." (5.5.13) The metaphor is echoed by Malcolm who calls Macbeth a "dead butcher." (5.9.36) The presentation of Macbeth as killing and feasting on dead bodies is contrasted with Malcolm who invokes the "grace of Grace" (5.9.39) to enable him to reassert "measure, time, and place." (5.9.40) Again, Shakespeare clearly juxtaposes the good legitimate monarch with the evil illegitimate tyrant Macbeth. Where Macbeth brings chaos, Malcolm brings calm and order.

Thus, Shakespeare presents the defeat of good at the hands of the evil tyrant Macbeth. The country plunges into disorder and horror and, as Lady Macduff realises, only by being evil can someone thrive. Ultimately, encouraged and funded by the saintly King Edward, Malcolm and Macduff are able to employ violence to return good to Scotland. Shakespeare suggests that violence itself is not evil if used for good and the decapitation of Macbeth is celebrated as a just punishment for such an evil man.

10: Essay Writing Checklist

As you read, check how many of the recommendations below are followed by the essay. Then, use the checklist to help you write your own essay.

Remember that these are *recommendations* from an experienced teacher, not *requirements*. Allow them to help and guide you, but don't allow them to restrict you; if you have a different idea and feel confident about it, then give it a go!

- ☐ Use wording of question in answer – "Shakespeare presents."
- ☐ Use Intro and Conclusion to help structure essay as argument.
- ☐ Use topic sentences to open each main paragraph.
- ☐ Close focus on extract.
- ☐ Focus on elsewhere in the play.
- ☐ Use short, precise quotations to support interpretations.
- ☐ Close analysis of language, especially aspects of poetry.
- ☐ Close analysis of form, especially aspects of performance.
- ☐ Close analysis of text structure, especially aspects of tragedy.
- ☐ Refer to effect on audience.
- ☐ Use relevant subject terminology.
- ☐ Connect to context when text was written, where relevant: Jacobean era.
- ☐ Connect to context when text is set, where relevant: early medieval Scotland.
- ☐ Connect to literary context, where relevant: history of the genre of tragedy.
- ☐ Connect to original and 21st century audience context, where relevant.
- ☐ Focus on minor character(s), where relevant.
- ☐ Use accurate spelling, punctuation and grammar.
- ☐ Write c450-c750 words.

11: Natural and unnatural

Read the following extract from Act 2 Scene 4 of *Macbeth* and then answer the question that follows.

At this moment in the play, Ross and an Old Man discuss the current situation in Scotland.

ROSS
Ha, good father,
Thou seest the heavens, as troubled with man's act,
Threatens his bloody stage. By th'clock 'tis day
And yet dark night strangles the travelling lamp.
Is't night's predominance, or the day's shame,
That darkness does the face of earth entomb
When living light should kiss it?
OLD MAN
'Tis unnatural,
Even like the deed that's done. On Tuesday last,
A falcon tow'ring in her pride of place
Was by a mousing owl hawk'd at and kill'd.
ROSS
And Duncan's horses, a thing most strange and certain,
Beauteous and swift, the minions of their race,
Turn'd wild in nature, broke their stalls, flung out,
Contending 'gainst obedience as they would
Make war with mankind.
OLD MAN
'Tis said, they eat each other.

Starting with this moment, explore how Shakespeare presents ideas about natural and unnatural in *Macbeth*.

Write about:

- how Shakespeare presents ideas about natural and unnatural at this moment in the play

- how Shakespeare presents ideas about natural and unnatural in the play as a whole.

11: The Essay

In *Macbeth*, Shakespeare presents nature as an ordered system that can be undermined by unnatural actions. Macbeth's usurpation of the throne is presented as an unnatural act and sends the natural world into confusion. Some characters in the play are presented as naturally evil or good; other characters are presented as calling on supernatural beings to help them change their character. As the play progresses, the dividing line between what is natural and what is unnatural becomes blurred, and only after much violence and death is 'natural order' restored.

In the extract, Shakespeare shows Ross and the Old Man exclaiming at shocking events in the natural world. Ross questions why "darkness does the face of earth entomb." (2.4.9) The chilling personification suggests that the earth is dead and has been buried by the darkness. This could be merely an unusually dark day, but the Old Man makes an explicit connection to the murder of Duncan, calling the darkness "unnatural, even like the deed that's done." (2.4.10-11) This shows that Ross and the Old Man interpret these troubling events in the natural world as reflections of the recent troubling 'deed' in the world of Scottish politics. Perhaps they may go even further and believe the events are *directly caused* by the recent regicide as the description of Duncan's horses, "turn'd wild in nature" (2.4.16) and going on to "eat each other" (2.4.18) suggests that the horses are reacting consciously to the death of their erstwhile rider. These reactions are perhaps a reflection of how, in the era before modern science, people tried to explain apparently inexplicable natural events as reflections of sinful human actions. Indeed, many of Shakespeare's original audience would have interpreted the omens witnessed by Ross and the Old Man as signs of God's displeasure at the disordering of his Creation.

Earlier in the play, Shakespeare presents Macbeth and Lady Macbeth challenging nature. Macbeth's reaction to the Witches' prophecies is "against the use of nature." (1.3.136) His beating heart and unfixed hair are physical manifestations of Macbeth's apparently unnatural desire to be king. Lady Macbeth, knowing her husband well, understands that Macbeth's true "nature" (1.5.15) is in fact "too full o'th'milk of human kindness." (1.5.16) Her metaphor presents Macbeth's nature as nurturing and 'unmasculine' and, for Lady Macbeth, this presents a problem as she requires Macbeth to be brutal. She also needs this of herself and, calling on supernatural aid to fill her with "direst cruelty" (1.5.42), she understands she must be "unsex[ed]" (1.5.40) and resist any "compunctious visitings of nature" (1.5.44) that might encourage her to remorse and 'feminine' compassion. For the protagonists, nature's tendency towards kindness and loyalty, as they see it, is an obstacle to their ambitions. Moreover, Shakespeare presents nature as defining fixed gender roles, suggesting that Macbeth and Lady Macbeth are also 'unnatural' because they defy the traditional attitudes of their era.

Later in the play, Shakespeare presents the re-assertion of natural order. In England, Malcolm tests Macduff's loyalty by confessing a litany of character "taints" (4.3.124) before revealing that these flaws are in fact "strangers to [his] nature." (4.3.125) Macduff's anguish at Malcolm's apparent sinful nature emphasises that Macduff believes that the true nature of a king should be one of wisdom and compassion. The contrast with Macbeth's unnatural behaviour is clear and Malcolm, having revealed his true character, is presented as the rightful King of Scots. In Scotland, meanwhile, Lady Macbeth is tormented by her conscience. Her doctor diagnoses her compulsive behaviour as the result of "unnatural deeds" (5.1.63) that "breed unnatural troubles." (5.1.64) We can interpret her deterioration to be part of the tragic downfall in the play. Macbeth, the tragic hero, also falls, fittingly aided by apparent distortions of nature – the moving of Birnham Wood and Macduff's "untimely" birth. (5.8.16) While Macbeth believes these to be unnatural, the audience can understand these to be natural, results of good army tactics and good midwifery. It is Macbeth, the illegitimate usurper who is presented as unnatural. Malcolm's stately proclamation of "measure, time and place" (5.9.40) demonstrates that natural order has been restored and the horror of Macbeth's unnatural rule is over.

Thus, Shakespeare presents a story of characters who challenge the natural order and achieve stunning success. However, though initially destabilised, the natural order strikes back and purges the unnatural irritants, bringing peace and legitimate rule back to Scotland. This message may be difficult for modern audiences, used more liberal attitudes about what is 'natural' and what is 'unnatural.' For Shakespeare, and for his original audience, there clearly were no such qualms. For them, the boundaries were clear and the correct punishment for transgression, for being 'unnatural,' was death.

11: Essay Writing Checklist

As you read, check how many of the recommendations below are followed by the essay. Then, use the checklist to help you write your own essay.

Remember that these are *recommendations* from an experienced teacher, not *requirements*. Allow them to help and guide you, but don't allow them to restrict you; if you have a different idea and feel confident about it, then give it a go!

- [ ] Use wording of question in answer – "Shakespeare presents."
- [ ] Use Intro and Conclusion to help structure essay as argument.
- [ ] Use topic sentences to open each main paragraph.
- [ ] Close focus on extract.
- [ ] Focus on elsewhere in the play.
- [ ] Use short, precise quotations to support interpretations.
- [ ] Close analysis of language, especially aspects of poetry.
- [ ] Close analysis of form, especially aspects of performance.
- [ ] Close analysis of text structure, especially aspects of tragedy.
- [ ] Refer to effect on audience.
- [ ] Use relevant subject terminology.
- [ ] Connect to context when text was written, where relevant: Jacobean era.
- [ ] Connect to context when text is set, where relevant: early medieval Scotland.
- [ ] Connect to literary context, where relevant: history of the genre of tragedy.
- [ ] Connect to original and 21st century audience context, where relevant.
- [ ] Focus on minor character(s), where relevant.
- [ ] Use accurate spelling, punctuation and grammar.
- [ ] Write c450-c750 words.

12: Guilt

Read the following extract from Act 2 Scene 2 of *Macbeth* and then answer the question that follows.

At this moment in the play, Macbeth has just killed King Duncan but can't face returning to plant the daggers with the dead guards.

LADY MACBETH
Infirm of purpose!
Give me the daggers. The sleeping and the dead
Are but as pictures; 'tis the eye of childhood
That fears a painted devil. If he do bleed,
I'll gild the faces of the grooms withal,
For it must seem their guilt.
[Exit.
Knock within
MACBETH
Whence is that knocking?
How is't with me, when every noise appals me?
What hands are here? Ha: they pluck out mine eyes.
Will all great Neptune's ocean wash this blood
Clean from my hand? No, this my hand will rather
The multitudinous seas incarnadine,
Making the green one red.
Enter Lady Macbeth
LADY MACBETH
My hands are of your colour, but I shame
To wear a heart so white.
Knock within
I hear a knocking
At the south entry. Retire we to our chamber;
A little water clears us of this deed.
How easy is it, then! Your constancy
Hath left you unattended.

Starting with this moment, explore how Shakespeare presents guilt in *Macbeth*.

Write about:

- how Shakespeare presents guilt at this moment in the play
- how Shakespeare presents guilt in the play as a whole.

12: The Essay

In *Macbeth*, Shakespeare presents guilt as causing extreme mental and physical degradation and eventually leading to Macbeth and Lady Macbeth's deaths. Though initially they try to either dismiss or manage their guilt, by the end of the play both are so consumed with guilt that they break down and their regime collapses. Shakespeare also presents Macduff's guilt at not being able to protect his family from being murdered; he is shown using this guilt to drive him to revenge.

In the extract, Shakespeare presents guilt as causing Macbeth to break down. Lady Macbeth remains calm, commanding her husband ("Give me the daggers." 2.2.56) and ensuring that evidence is planted on the grooms so that "it must seem their guilt." (2.2.60) At this point, for Lady Macbeth, guilt is merely another aspect of her plan that she needs to manage. She sees guilt only as something to be feigned, much like the distress she is already planning to feign when the news of Duncan's death is revealed. Macbeth, by comparison, is reduced to a wreck of despair and guilt. Trying to wash the blood from his hands he realises that his hand "will rather the multitudinous seas incarnadine, making the green one red." (2.2.64-66) His blood and his guilt, he feels, will taint even the largest oceans. The precipitous fall from Latinate poetry, using words ("multitudinous" "incarnadine") that may well have been coined by Shakespeare, to direct simple language here ("green" "red") perhaps reflects what will be Macbeth's own trajectory: from majesty to nothing. Lady Macbeth, by comparison, shrugs off this, to her eyes, foolish emoting: "a little water clears us of this deed." (2.2.70) She takes Macbeth's water metaphor and renders it concrete. Water will indeed wash away the blood but not, the audience understands, the guilt.

As the play progresses, Shakespeare shows Macbeth continually wracked by guilt. He demonstrates his turbulent mental state when he exclaims: "full of scorpions is my mind." (3.2.36) This startling metaphor suggests that Macbeth's mind is poisoned, by fear and by guilt. Later, at the feast, Macbeth is tormented by Banquo's ghost who is presented, to the audience, as a visual representation of Macbeth's guilt. Lady Macbeth's reaction to the ghost, however, shows that she still feels no guilt; she dismisses Macbeth's behaviour as more suited for a "woman's story at a winter's fire." (3.4.65) Here, she attacks Macbeth for his perceived unmanliness, suggesting that feeling guilt is weak and feminine. Having previously disavowed her own femininity (1.5.40), rejecting the traditional gender roles of her era, Lady Macbeth clearly feels that a powerful man would not feel guilty. Macbeth, though, having shamed himself before the most powerful men in the kingdom, is rapidly losing power and now cannot stop contemplating his likely punishment. "Blood will have blood," (3.4.122) is his interpretation of the ghost's visitation. Macbeth believes that his bloody crime will be repaid by another bloody crime. Perhaps he foresees his death at this point, aware that his guilt will never leave him.

Later, Shakespeare presents guilt serving as a positive inspiration for the forces of good. Macduff is grief-stricken upon hearing of his family's horrifying deaths, believing they were killed "not for their own demerits but for mine." (4.3.229) He interprets his family's deaths as being partly his own fault, perhaps feeling that, had he stayed in Scotland, his family may have lived. Malcolm encourages Macduff to convert this guilt to action: "be this the whetstone of your sword." (4.3.231) The metaphor presents Macduff's guilt as the tool that will sharpen his sword, ready for revenge. This may also reflect Malcolm's own guilt for, after all, he too chose to flee. By contrast, Lady Macbeth sleepwalks, wracked by her guilt; seeing her speaking in disjointed prose, her mind flitting from idea to idea, causes the shocked Doctor to mutter that "unnatural deeds do breed unnatural troubles." (5.1.63-64) He witnesses Lady Macbeth's "infected mind" (5.1.64) and understands the truth; she is guilty, not sick, and he diagnoses her need to confess to a priest. Many of the Protestant Christians in the original audience would have rejected this idea, perhaps seeing it as part of Shakespeare's depiction of the strange superstitious world of medieval Scotland, happily swept away by Malcolm's victory.

Thus, Shakespeare presents guilt as a powerful force that visits retribution on the guilty. They are torn apart mentally and physically, seeing the world around them destroyed. Only through virtuous actions, it is suggested, can guilt be absolved and turned to the good. Macbeth and Lady Macbeth, filled with evil and resisting all compunction, never attain absolution and receive instead the deserved punishment of the evil sinner – death and eternal damnation.

12: Essay Writing Checklist

As you read, check how many of the recommendations below are followed by the essay. Then, use the checklist to help you write your own essay.

Remember that these are *recommendations* from an experienced teacher, not *requirements*. Allow them to help and guide you, but don't allow them to restrict you; if you have a different idea and feel confident about it, then give it a go!

☐	Use wording of question in answer – "Shakespeare presents."	☐	Refer to effect on audience.
☐	Use Intro and Conclusion to help structure essay as argument.	☐	Use relevant subject terminology.
☐	Use topic sentences to open each main paragraph.	☐	Connect to context when text was written, where relevant: Jacobean era.
☐	Close focus on extract.	☐	Connect to context when text is set, where relevant: early medieval Scotland.
☐	Focus on elsewhere in the play.	☐	Connect to literary context, where relevant: history of the genre of tragedy.
☐	Use short, precise quotations to support interpretations.	☐	Connect to original and 21st century audience context, where relevant.
☐	Close analysis of language, especially aspects of poetry.	☐	Focus on minor character(s), where relevant.
☐	Close analysis of form, especially aspects of performance.	☐	Use accurate spelling, punctuation and grammar.
☐	Close analysis of text structure, especially aspects of tragedy.	☐	Write c450-c750 words.

Appendix 1: How will my essay be assessed?

In your AQA GCSE English Literature exams, the *Macbeth* task will count for 21% of your total marks so practising essay writing is absolutely vital and can make a huge difference to your final grade.

How will my essay be assessed?

The exam board will assess your essay by checking to see how far you have met the four Assessment Objectives:

AO1	Read, understand and respond to texts. Students should be able to: • maintain a critical style and develop an informed personal response • use textual references, including quotations, to support and illustrate interpretations.
AO2	Analyse the language, form and structure used by a writer to create meanings and effects, using relevant subject terminology where appropriate.
AO3	Show understanding of the relationships between texts and the contexts in which they were written.
AO4	Use a range of vocabulary and sentence structures for clarity, purpose and effect, with accurate spelling and punctuation.

This exam board language, however, can feel a bit technical or vague. After all, what is a "critical style"? Who decides what is "appropriate" and what isn't?

(Answers: a critical style means that your essay should demonstrate its conclusions by using evidence from the text. Don't simply tell the examiner that Macbeth is violent; prove it using evidence from the text. And: it is your examiner, ultimately, who will decide what is appropriate and what isn't.)

Rather than answering these questions theoretically, the essays in this book aim to show in practical terms how it's possible to give your examiner what they are looking for, within the time constraints of the exam, whilst showing off the full range of your text knowledge and writing technique.

What makes these essays excellent exam essays?

It is true that there are many ways to organise information in an essay and you, or your teacher, may have different preferences about how to approach writing these essays. The essays in this book reflect my judgement of what is the best approach based on my professional knowledge of what works for my students, my knowledge of what is readily readable by examiners and, perhaps most importantly, my own experience of writing these essays under timed conditions.

The twelve essays here follow a consistent pattern:

- an Introduction paragraph outlining in summary the answer to the essay question.
- three detailed Main Paragraphs offering a critical analysis, first of the extract and subsequently other parts of the play, providing evidence to back up my answer. These paragraphs also include, where relevant, connections to the text's contexts.
- a final Conclusion paragraph offering a re-statement of the essay answer in summary form with, where relevant, connections to the resonance of the text for modern audiences.

This pattern can be learned and repeated, making it an excellent tool for students. It is achievable under the times constraints of the exam. Finally, the pattern is also clear, readable and, importantly, familiar to examiners which means you are not requiring your examiners to interpret a more muddled, inconsistent structure.

Each essay shows:

- a critical style based on my own understanding of the text.
- textual references (usually short quotations embedded into sentences) used to support interpretations.

- analysis of how Shakespeare uses language (especially poetry), form (the text's nature as a play) and structure (especially aspects of tragedy) to create meanings and effects.
- relevant subject terminology used where appropriate.
- understanding of the relationship between the text and its contexts (including, where relevant, references to when the text was written and first performed, when the text was set and when the text is performed in the modern day).
- a range of vocabulary, varied sentence structures, accurate spelling, consistent punctuation and clear grammar.

Finally, these essays are short – around 750 words. The first drafts were written under the same conditions as the ones you will face (50-55 minutes for the AQA exam) and therefore reflect what is possible in such a short time. You may initially find it difficult to write so much detail in such a short space of time, but regular practice will definitely enable you to improve.

Best of luck in your exams!

Printed in Great Britain
by Amazon

38581802R00040